KINGDOM *Legacy*

A Father-Daughter Anointing

SARAH DAVIS

Kingdom Legacy: A Father-Daughter Anointing

ISBNs: 978-0-578-34363-1 (Print)

978-0-578-34526-0 (Ebook)

Printed in the United States of America.

I dedicate this book to my mother and father who have poured into my life and made me the woman I am today.

Contents

The mantle has fallen!

He [Elisha] also took up the mantle of Elijah that had fallen from him, and went back and stood by the bank of the Jordan. (2 Kings 2:13, addition mine)

Foreword

Some people come into your life for a season and others for a reason. Sarah and her father, Alex, have been part of my life for as long as I can remember. I can't adequately express in this short space the many ways they have blessed me throughout the years.

Some may call me a special case. I would like to think that I am, but the truth is that they treat everyone the same way. The love, care, concern, and respect they show all people is unparalleled. That is why I believe the words (and revelation) you are about to read will truly impact your life. Each chapter is handcrafted and flowing from true love for the body of Christ. This book has been a long time in the making. It points us to how important it is to not let the Enemy use the generational gap to divide us. Wisdom is always there to be gleaned from one another, no matter how old or young.

A *legacy* is defined as a gift passed down. I believe the gifts in this book will not go only to you, but will be given to generations to come as well, as a truly multi-generational tool to equip the army of the Lord.

There has never been a point in time when we have needed this resource more. The writing of history itself has been attacked in our time. In fact, people have even attempted to erase it. Within these pages, you will learn the importance of listening to the wisdom of our elders. It is through this process that we can run with accurate vision to the next place the Lord is leading us. *Kingdom Legacy* is a beautiful picture of not just a father/daughter anointing, but of God the Father's heart for all of His precious children. Get ready. You're next to take the torch!

—*Catherine Stewart*
WOW Ministries

Introduction

The inspiration for this book came from a box of sermon notes my father gave me from his forty years in ministry as a pastor. I have dedicated this book to both my parents because they taught me the ways of the Lord. Great has been my peace as a result. My mother's unconditional love and patience mixed with my father's revelation knowledge has been the firm foundation upon which my life has been built. Blessed with the finest parents ever, I will be forever grateful to my heavenly Father for them. They were a perfect mix. Once, the Holy Spirit impressed on me that He put everything in my mother that my father lacked and vice versa—and then He gave me to them. I got a double portion! Double for your trouble.

My mother is with Jesus now, but while writing this my father moved in with me, and I purchased our dream home in Manassas, Virginia. One day as we were driving downtown in Manassas, my dad pointed to a church and told me it was the one in which my brother and sister were baptized forty years prior. I am the youngest of four. Mary and Alex, the twins, were eleven years older than me, and my brother James was two years older than me. All three of their lives were cut short by tragedy.

At that moment, I realized the Lord had brought my family full circle in forty years. The journey had begun in Manassas, and now, forty years later, we found ourselves right back where we had started. *This was our promised land.* If we had known back then what was ahead of us, I don't think we could have borne it. It's no wonder that the good Lord takes us one step at a time. After our great losses, all of us, even my mother who was the glue of the family, went through seasons of depression in which we felt dry and alone. But God had a plan, and in spite of all that happened in their lives, my parents left a legacy to all the people they touched throughout those forty years, especially me.

In the Bible, an elderly Jacob blesses his grandsons, Ephraim and Manasseh, the sons of Joseph. The name *Manasseh* means "to forget." God had brought him to a place where he could forget all the troubles and hurt of his past. I used to think that was not possible. I lived with a lot of guilt and shame. *Ephraim* means to "be fruitful in the land of affliction." The city of Manassas (it was originally Manassa; the "s" was added later) was our place of promise. It may have taken forty years of wandering, but in "the land of forget-my-affliction" I have found my fruitful place. You see, if you forgive yourself and others, the Lord will bless you and help you forget the pain. In this place, the hand of God has blessed me.

Now when Joseph saw that his father laid his right hand on the head of Ephraim, it displeased him; so he took hold of his father's hand to remove it from Ephraim's head to Manasseh's head. And Joseph said to his father, "Not so, my father, for this one is the firstborn; put your right hand on his head." But his father refused and said, "I know, my son, I know. He also shall become a people, and he also shall be great; but truly his younger brother shall be greater than he, and his descendants shall become a multitude of nations." So he blessed them that day, saying, "By you Israel will bless, saying, 'May God make you as Ephraim and as Manasseh!' " And thus he set Ephraim before Manasseh. Then Israel said to Joseph, "Behold, I am dying, but God will be with you and bring you back to the land of your fathers. Moreover I have given to you one portion above your brothers, which I took from the hand of the Amorite with my sword and my bow." (Genesis 48:17-22)

Chapter 1: Kingdom Legacy 101

> I have fought the good fight, I have finished the race, I have kept the faith. (2 Timothy 4:7)

A *kingdom legacy* refers to our lives in the Big Picture from God's perspective. Sometimes we struggle, thinking, *God, what are You doing now?* That's when we remember He has the whole race mapped out ahead of us. He is at the finish line. There is a generation that will continue the race and carry the baton further based on the choices we determine today. Remember this is a not a sprint, but a marathon. We don't run this race on our own. We run with God and He gives us the grace to finish well.

This book is a series of eight lessons followed by a prophetic call that I believe goes out to all those God has called to walk in His kingdom authority and wisdom in this time. Of course, that call is for *all* who belong to Him. However, before we get to that, it is important that we assimilate some important truths.

The sheer volume of information that accosts us daily is staggering when compared to even twenty years ago. Therefore, it is vital that we are well-grounded in what God—Creator and Master of the Universe—has to say about who we are and our purpose here. No other subject is closer to His heart. His desire is for all people, and each of us fits into His plan to reach them. As with all plans, though, it has a strong foundation, and that is the subject of this chapter.

There are three points that are key to you walking in your kingdom legacy:

1. Know your *identity.*
2. Find your *voice.*
3. Walk in *authority.*

Who Are You?

Identity theft is rampant today. People are constantly being robbed by someone who is pretending to be them. But this is not the worst identity theft going on. Since the very beginning, the Devil has put his greatest efforts into stealing your identity. He actually runs his kingdom by messing with your identity. Why? Because he knows that if you know your true identity and comprehend it well, you will step into your proper place as a child of God. If you do that, it is game over for him.

The majority of people in the world struggle with their identity. They question and search—sometimes for their entire lives. They ask: Who am I? Why am I here? What is my purpose?

If a man or woman does not know who he or she is, they are in danger of becoming someone else. If a father doesn't tell his children who they are, they will always try to identify with someone else. My father taught me about my place in the kingdom from birth, but I still struggled with identity. *There is a difference between knowing and believing your identity.*

The very first thing God gave Adam was *His image*. If you remember, He said, "Let Us make man in Our image" in Genesis 1.

Our image is also the image of the Father, the Son, and the Holy Ghost.

We are living in a culture in which people regularly identify with just about anything. One day a person may identify as a man, one day a woman, one day a lobster. (Just kidding.) The point is that the Enemy is running roughshod over people everywhere because they don't know their identity in the Lord. Meanwhile the Devil is having a field day, laughing.

We must appropriate God's truths. We are called and chosen into the kingdom of God to rise up as warriors—mighty men or women of valor. We are fishers of men. You are either a man of integrity or a valuable woman; both are full of the beauty of God within. We are a chosen generation, a royal priesthood, called like Joshua to take back everything the Enemy has stolen so we can defeat all of his demons and lies. It is time we began prophesying truth over ourselves.

We must appropriate God's truths about ourselves so that we can withstand the confusion of our times and move out to fulfil our purpose too.

To begin this process, I made a list of "I Am" statements. Read these aloud every day until you start believing them. I did. This list will get you started. Add to it.

I am forgiven.

I am chosen.

I am confident.

I am fearless.

I am wanted.

I am loved.

I am enough.

I am *more* than enough.

I am royalty.

I am a King's kid.

I am strong.

I am created uniquely.

I am born with purpose.

I am anointed.

Let God minister even more detailed statements that define who you are. Put your list in a journal and read it aloud to yourself daily. (Remember, faith comes by hearing!) Doing this will cement these truths into your heart and soul. Knowing who we are is the foundation for everything else we ever do.

Speak Up!

The "quiet one" is a term that was used to identify me for years. When I was four years old, my sister, Mary, crossed over to glory. Mary was fifteen years young. I have a vivid memory of my parents and eldest brother coming home from the hospital that day. My aunt was my main caregiver at the time because my mom and dad spent countless days and nights at hospitals. My aunt was rushing to get my and my brother's shoes tied. All of sudden, the front door opened. It is burned into my mind. I saw my parents' beaten and drained faces. The only thing they uttered under their breath was, "She's gone." My aunt began to remove our shoes. I believe this was the moment that I hid my voice. I never lost it; I just hid it deep inside. I felt like I was covered with shame, hurt, and disappointment. This would be the first of many losses in my life.

Mary had been diagnosed with a brain tumor at the age of twelve. Both my brothers also died young. My brother Aly Boy choked on a "boneless" chicken wing in a barbecue restaurant, and my brother James did not wake up one morning when he was twenty-two. Their deaths hit our family hard. James and I were less than two years apart and were best friends. After burying three children, my mom also passed from a large mass in her lung. Then my husband died from an accident when he was thirty-five. My daughter was only ten and my son nearly two. Through all this I became numb inside. I didn't want to live anymore, and I prayed for God to take me. I was not suicidal, but I was very depressed, and these thoughts could have led to suicidal ones. Asking God to take you is not healthy, especially when you are raising two young children.

From that darkness, I began a journey to find out what I was supposed to do with my life. I am thankful that my parents had built into me an understanding of my identity, so that was one thing I did not have to wrestle with in addition to the pain in my soul.

I did not find my voice overnight; it took a long time. It was almost like God was unraveling my heart—one knot at a time. Years of hurt and disappointment take time to heal. God could have done it overnight, but in His loving tenderness, He patiently held my hand and walked with me. Little by little, I started to give it over to Him. One morning in the shower He spoke to my heart and said, "Open your mouth. Being quiet is killing you." Wow! I had no idea it was that serious.

I thought my silence was part of who I was—a strength and not a weakness. This quietness had become a great stronghold in my life. A stronghold is a lie you have believed too long. You find yourself trapped in a fortress, not able to see the truth behind the great walls you have built in your mind. (This is just one more reason that we know who we really are in Christ.)

The truth was that I had not lost my voice; it was just hidden. My quietness was a defense mechanism; in fact, my voice was my defense (my shield) and had been all along. I began to have praise and worship sessions with the Lord alone. Just me and Him. Real talks about how I was truly feeling. I brought it *all* to the table. There was repentance on the floor. Then came the moment that changed my life forever.

A mentor of mine insisted quite intently that a minister pray for me for the baptism of the Holy Ghost. Timid and a little nervous, he asked me if I had ever spoken in tongues. I said, "No…well, there was this one time twenty years ago at a prayer room. I had for a minute, but I didn't think it was real and stopped immediately." He told me I had believed a lie. It was real. He asked if I remembered the words. I thought, *Remember the words? That was twenty years ago!* He began to pray that the Lord would bring them back. God did just that. The exact words came back to my remembrance and I began to flow with rivers of living water. I felt a burning (yes, an actual burning) in my spirit for days. That was the moment I started the wildest ride of my life, and I am still on it. I had discovered my kingdom voice!

Walking in Authority

As I started to discover and walk in my kingdom authority, the Holy Spirit impressed on me to write myself a letter from God. He told me not to overthink it, but to just write how God viewed me. In my first book, there was a chapter, "Never Underestimate the Persistent Widow." As I sat down to write, God gave me a name change. This is the letter.

> Dear Persistent Warrior,
>
> I am so proud of you. You are taking back ground and advancing My kingdom. Do not stop now. I am giving you everywhere your foot treads. The kingdom of hell is shaken and in terror every time your foot hits the ground. Keep going forward. Thank you for always trusting in Me. You have never doubted for a second that I would not be with you. Great is your faithfulness. Anything you lack, you can borrow from My never-ending storehouse. All things shall be given unto you. I hold back nothing from you. Just hold on to My staying power. I will be with you till the end of time.
>
> Your Partner in the kingdom,
>
> Yahweh

Just as I said before, there is a difference between knowing your identity and believing it. There is also a difference between knowing your authority and *walking in* your authority. God has given you the keys to the kingdom. Jesus delivered the kingdom to us and made it available, so we have the keys and access to the doors to enter spiritual realms. We can go where no man has gone before. We have been given dominion over the earth. The Enemy has been defeated once and for all by our Savior Jesus Christ, but… Yes, the dreaded "but." But the Enemy is god of this world (little "g"), and he is seeking whom he may devour. It is our job to keep him in his place—under our feet. We must do this. We are the Warrior Army. God has been waiting for us to rise up, preach the kingdom to all the nations, and walk in our God-given and God-directed authority. True warriors don't have multitudes of privates and corporals. True warriors empower more warrior leaders. We don't break ranks. We also don't fight like unbelievers. We war in the Spirit. We unleash heaven on earth. We don't play patty-cake with demonic forces. We cast them out. They have to submit to the name and blood of Jesus. When we open our mouths, miracles, power, and revelation come bursting out. Out of all the gifts, Paul highlighted prophecy.

> Pursue love, and desire spiritual gifts, but especially that you may prophesy. (1 Corinthians 14:1)

Why? I believe it is because the prophetic voice of the body of Christ reflect the "now words" from God. What is God speaking *now?* This is why the prophetic voice is always attacked the most. The Enemy wants to silence and discredit every prophetic voice. We have *all* been called to prophesy; it is an essential part of walking in our kingdom authority. We are not all called to hold the office of prophet, but to prophesy is a function of the Spirit through all of us. There is a difference. The Bible says, "Your sons and daughters will prophesy!" You have the signet ring.

> So the king took off his signet ring, which he had taken from Haman, and gave it to Mordecai; and Esther appointed Mordecai over the house of Haman. (Esther 8:2)

Who is making the decrees now? You are—as your enemy hangs from the gallows. Perhaps you, like Esther, have come into the kingdom "for such a time as this" (Esther 4:14). You have God's permission and authority to fight and annihilate the Enemy.

Today is the day you receive the baton to run your race. You will take the kingdom further than before. Every generation's ceiling is the next generation's floor. He lifts us higher and higher. Step into the kingdom legacy that was set in motion for you before the foundation of the earth. Your Father in heaven sat at your end, stepped back to your beginning, and walked with you every step of the way. Now is the time to put on your running shoes. This is not the trend, the mainstream, or the modern system. You are part of a kingdom legacy. And this is the Father/Child Anointing you were born to walk in!

Chapter 2: Woman, Free at Last!

Women in ministry has become one of the most controversial subjects the church has faced for centuries. I'd like to look at this subject scripturally and put it on trial. Because, why not?

That controversy is over the woman's place in ministry.

Let's take the two scriptures that are the basis for the controversy and put them on trial. We'll call witnesses, but *you* are the jury. Let's allow the Holy Spirit to have His perfect work in us. So eyes wide open, hearts ready and pliable, let's go!

All rise as the honorable Holy Spirit enters the room. You may be seated.

The two Scriptures on trial today are:

> And I do not permit a woman to teach or to have authority over a man, but to be in silence.(1 Timothy 2:12)

> Let your women keep silent in the churches, for they are not permitted to speak; but they are to be submissive, as the law also says. (1 Corinthians 14:34)

We call witnesses as directed by a few other verses:

> But if he will not hear, take with you one or two more, that "by the mouth of two or three witnesses every word may be established." (Matthew 18:16)

> Do not receive an accusation against an elder except from two or three witnesses. (1 Timothy 5:19)

> Whoever is deserving of death shall be put to death on the testimony of two or three witnesses; he shall not be put to death on the testimony of one witness. (Deuteronomy 17:6)

These verses cover the subject of "witnesses" in both the Old and the New Testaments and clearly outline the importance of calling on witnesses (the Word of God) as we will be doing today. We want to get to the truth and see what the apostle Paul really meant. Keep in mind that the truth will *always* sets you free and *never* put you in handcuffs.

As our first witness, we will call Adam. (We literally have to start at the beginning with this one.)

> And the Lord God formed man of the dust of the ground, and breathed into his nostrils the breath of life; and man became a living being. (Genesis 2:7)

> And the Lord God said, "It is not good that man should be alone; I will make him a helper comparable to him." (Genesis 2:18)

The *King James Version* uses the word *helpmeet*, which means "to join, to match, to contend successfully with, and in harmony and agreement."

> Then the rib which the Lord God had taken from man He made into a woman, and He brought her to the man. And Adam said: "This is now bone of my bones and flesh of my flesh; she shall be called Woman, because she was taken out of Man." Therefore a man shall leave his father and mother and be joined to his wife, and they shall become one flesh. (Genesis 2:22-24)

One Flesh

The *King James Version* says that man shall "cleave unto his wife." The definition of *cleave* is "to adhere firmly and closely or loyally and unwaveringly."

Note how it says the man's job is to cleave (adhere firmly and closely or loyally and unwaveringly) unto his wife.

Did I hear a man scream, "Objection"?

OK, overruled, let's move on.

Let's look at Genesis 5:

> Male and female created he them; and blessed them, and called their name Adam, in the day when they were created. (Genesis 5:2 KJV)

God called *their* name Adam. Both of them! When He wanted the man He called, "Adam!" and when He wanted the woman He called "Adam!" It wasn't until after the fall that woman was called Eve.

Let's talk about names for a minute. With a name comes character recognition. For instance, when we say the name of *God*, we think of how He is all-knowing, all-powerful, the Beginning and the End, and more. When we say the name of *Jesus*, we think of Love poured out, the sacrificial Lamb, and the Lion of Judah. When we say *Abraham Lincoln*, we think of a great president. When we say *Rockefeller*, we think of great wealth. You may say (insert your name here) and think set free, delivered, daughter (or son) of the Most High

God! Know your identity, know your name. Know your authority.

God has given *you* dominion over all the earth.

> And God said, Let us make man in our image, after our likeness: and let them have dominion over the fish of the sea, and over the fowl of the air, and over the cattle, and over all the earth, and over every creeping thing that creepeth upon the earth. (Genesis 1:26 KJV)

He said, "Let *them* have dominion."

Dominion refers to "sovereignty or control" as in "man's attempt to establish dominion over nature."

When God said let *them* have dominion, there were only two people there: Adam. They are one, *one flesh,* according to Genesis 2:24.

So God gave *them* dominion, control, and authority over all the earth.

They were given the same name because they were equal in their dominion.

Even though we were given authority on the earth, *we* sometimes make bad choices and exercise poor judgement. We shouldn't blame God. He gave *us* control over the earth. Even today, we do this constantly. We sit around doing nothing, or we allow the Enemy to deceive us when we have been given authority over him. However, God is good and His unending love *always* makes a way for us. It's up to us to grab hold of it and take it. Eve's bad choice cost a lot and Adam's response wasn't good either.

But we *must* understand our God's heart and character if we want to get close to His will.

Remember, the two scriptures on trial today are:

> And I do not permit a woman to teach or to have authority over a man, but to be in silence. (1 Timothy 2:12)

> Let your women keep silent in the churches, for they are not permitted to speak; but they are to be submissive, as the law also says. (1 Corinthians 14:34)

I encourage you to read all of 1 Corinthians 14 in its entirety too. For now, let's look at verses 27 and 28.

> If any man speak in an unknown tongue, let it be by two, or at the most by three, and that by course; and let one interpret. But if there be no interpreter, let him keep silence in the church; and let him speak to himself, and to God. (1 Corinthians 14:27-28 KJV)

Now Paul is talking about everyone—male and female—remaining silent.

The point is that this chapter is all about order in the service.

> For God is not the author of confusion, but of peace, as in all churches of the saints. (1 Corinthians 14:33 KJV)

The church in Corinth was out of order. For one thing, the church was set up with the women on one side and the men on the other, so if a woman didn't understand something, she had to yell across to her husband to even ask a question. Paul was writing them to help that situation. In that time, women were not normally as well-educated as the men were, and most woman were homemakers. So when Paul writes that a woman should ask her husband at home, it was simply giving them practical advice so they didn't disrupt their meeting.

> Let your women keep silence in the churches: for it is not permitted unto them to speak; but they are commanded to be under obedience, as also saith the law. And if they will learn any thing, let them ask their husbands at home: for it is a shame for women to speak in the church. (1 Corinthians 14:34-35 KJV)

Are you ready? The very next verse is this:

> What? came the word of God out from you? or came it unto you only? (1 Corinthians 14:36 KJV)

Paul is clearly answering a question the Corinthians had asked him in this entire passage. He is repeating it back to them. He is saying, "This isn't one of our practices, so why are you doing this?"

This is a true mic-drop moment.

He answers their question in verse 36.

What? (It sounds like he is angry.) "Women, keep silent!" *What?*

Read it again.

> What? came the word of God out from you? or came it unto you only? (1 Corinthians 14:36 KJV)

Uh-oh.

Today, if we took keeping women silent in the church literally, the men would have to start teaching Sunday school and setting their alarms so they can lead intercessory prayer at 6 a.m. on the weekends. Shall I go on? You'd also have to tell your favorite female worship leader to take a seat. I don't know about you, but I've seen many mighty prophetic female prayer warriors, anointed worship leaders, and excellent teachers. I may know more women than men under this heading. This verse has handcuffed over half the church. The truth should *always* set you free, never put you in bondage.

In truth, when we look at the whole counsel of God, Scripture itself does not support the idea that women should not have the same freedom in ministry as men. Think about it. There's Deborah, Huldah, Hannah, and Abigail in the Old Testament. In the New Testament, we read about Phoebe and Dorcas and Priscilla and many others. God has used women throughout the church age to teach, preach, heal, encourage, and so much more in the body of Christ just as He has used men.

We need to take the key and unlock those handcuffs today. We need to live in the freedom of the truth of the Word of God. This is true whether you are male or female. Your walk and the choices you make will be affected by what you believe. Our actions are governed by our beliefs, so it is truly vital that we follow Christ in this as in all things.

Now to blow your minds, who do you think mentored the apostle Paul, the writer of these letters? Let's look.

> I commend unto you Phebe our sister, which is a servant of the church which is at Cenchrea: That ye receive her in the Lord, as becometh saints, and that ye assist her in whatsoever business she hath need of you: for she hath been a

> succourer of many, and of myself also. (Romans 16:1-2 KJV)

Phoebe—a woman. A deacon in the church. Succourer of many, including Paul. A succourer is a nurturer, and it means to feed or raise up like we do a baby. Phoebe was also entrusted by Paul to deliver the letter to the Romans.

Next verse:

> Greet Priscilla and Aquila my helpers in Christ Jesus. (Romans 16:3 KJV)

Priscilla was the wife of Aquila. Earlier mentions of them had Aquila's name listed first, but in this verse Paul mentioned the woman's name first. I wonder why? Perhaps she had become the dominant one? I know a lot of religious people are going to have an issue with that one, but it's OK. We women can handle it.

Final point.

> Husbands, love your wives, even as Christ also loved the church, and gave himself for it. (Ephesians 5:25 KJV)

Husbands are to love their wives as Christ loved the church. Christ loved us first and we respond to that love. Husbands are to love their wives, and the wives are to respond to that love. If men are not loving their wives as Christ loved the church, what do you think the wives' responses will be?

> For the husband is the head of the wife, even as Christ is the head of the church: and he is the saviour of the body. Therefore as the church is subject unto Christ, so let the wives be to their own husbands in every thing. (Ephesians 5:23-24 KJV)

This is not about a woman's movement or women empowering women. It should be men empowering women, not handcuffing them. This is how the Lord intended it to be from the beginning.

Mary Magdalene was a woman, and the first person to spread the good news that Jesus was alive!

The woman at the well was the first evangelist.

In the upper room on the day of Pentecost, the gifts of the Spirit did not only fall on the men.

Now it's your turn. I challenge you to do some research on your own. There are women judges, prophetesses, evangelists, deacons, and prayer warriors throughout both New and Old Testaments.

Do you still think women should be absolutely silent in church?

Always remember when studying the Word of God that it is alive and active. It should always bring you closer to the heart of God so that you can better understand the will of God. It is God's will that you prosper and be edified, exhorted, comforted, set free, and delivered. These are all the will of God for you, as He wants to give you a future and a hope.

Shame, guilt, confusion, and oppression are not the will of God. To be told to "be silent, shut your mouth, and sit in the corner" is *not* the will of God. I had been silent too long, and it was killing me.

Open your mouth! That's a command, not a suggestion.

> And he said unto them, Go ye into all the world, and preach the gospel to every creature (Mark 16:15 KJV)

So now I say to you, woman, you are *free* at last!

Chapter 3: Keys to the Kingdom

> The key of the house of David I will lay on his shoulder; so he shall open, and no one shall shut; and he shall shut, and no one shall open. (Isaiah 22:22)

God gives us the keys to open and shut doors. Man cannot stop what God has appointed. God will make a way and open the door. He does not even hide the key under the mat. No. Intruders could find it that way. He lays it right on *your* shoulder, so you and only you can walk through.

My father studied the kingdom of God for forty years. It is still his favorite subject by far. Being raised on the kingdom, I never realized until recently that not everyone knows that we have the keys. We have direct access to the kingdom at hand. Today is the day you gain entry and your annual pass, all in one. Everything we do pertains to the kingdom, so this is important. John the Baptist proclaimed this:

> Repent, for the kingdom of heaven is at hand! (Matthew 3:2)

I noticed an order to it: John the Baptist paved the way, preaching in the wilderness; he baptized Jesus; Jesus was then tempted by Satan; John the Baptist went to jail; and Jesus began His Galilean ministry, at which point it says this:

> From that time Jesus began to preach and to say, "Repent, for the kingdom of heaven is at hand." (Matthew 4:17)

From that time on. What time on? Look at the verse before it.

> The people who sat in darkness have seen a great light, and upon those who sat in the region and shadow of death Light has dawned. (Matthew 4:16)

Thank You, Lord, they were seeing the light.

This was the order of things.

1. See the light.

Once you've seen the light, you don't want to go back to darkness. That's why the Enemy tries to keep you blinded and keep your love ones blinded. Sometimes it takes a Damascus Road experience like it did for Paul for us to see. Paul had a story, and we all have a story, a past. That's out testimony. The Enemy wants us to be ashamed and stay in our past, but the bigger the story, the bigger the past, the greater the glory!

2. Repent!

Turn around; you are going the *wrong* way. If you are waiting for a sign, here it is. Remember, repentance can refer to a change in direction or even a change in thinking.

3. Operate in the kingdom.

Listen, if you are waiting for the kingdom to come, or waiting to get to heaven to enter the kingdom, you are missing out. No, the kingdom of God is at hand. It is already here; it is inside of you, waiting for you to tap into it.

> Now when He was asked by the Pharisees when the kingdom of God would come, He answered them and said, "The

> kingdom of God does not come with observation; nor will they say, 'See here!' or 'See there!' For indeed, the kingdom of God is within you." (Luke 17:20-21)

We can operate in the kingdom right now on earth *as it is in heaven.*

The Lord's Prayer says, "Thy kingdom come, thy will be done on earth as it is in heaven."

> And I will give unto thee the keys of the kingdom of heaven: and whatsoever thou shalt bind on earth shall be bound in heaven: and whatsoever thou shalt loose on earth shall be loosed in heaven. (Matthew 16:19 KJV)

> Assuredly, I say to you, whatever you bind on earth will be bound in heaven, and whatever you loose on earth will be loosed in heaven. (Matthew 18:18)

We have the keys to the kingdom. Jesus said we have the keys to bind and to loose, as well as open and close doors in the spiritual realm. Let's take a minute and look at the meanings of those terms in *Strong's Exhaustive Concordance.*

The Greek word used here is *deó* and it means "to tie and bind," and in common usage it means to "bind, tie, fasten, impel, compel, and declare to be prohibited and unlawful.[1] The Greek word used for "loose" is *luó.* It means "to loose, to release, to dissolve" and in common usage it means "loose (unleash) let go; release (unbind) so something no longer holds together; and (figuratively) to release what has been held back (like Christ "releasing" the seven seals in the scroll in *Revelation*)."[2] These are powerful ideas.

To allow or to prohibit? What have you been allowing on earth?

Oooh, this just got real.

This is about the King's dominion-reign on earth as it is in heaven. Since man has dominion on earth, only we can bring down the King's dominion, and that's our job. We have access to it, but we should do it.

Man has dominion on earth. Let's read this verse one more time because it proves this point.

> And God said, Let us make man in our image, after our likeness: and let them have dominion over the fish of the sea, and over the fowl of the air, and over the cattle, and over all the earth, and over every creeping thing that creepeth upon the earth. (Genesis 1:26 KJV)

1. "G1210 - deō - Strong's Greek Lexicon (kjv)." Blue Letter Bible. Accessed 1 Dec, 2021. https://www.blueletterbible.org/lexicon/g1210/kjv/tr/0-1/.

2. "G3089 - lyō - Strong's Greek Lexicon (kjv)." Blue Letter Bible. Accessed 1 Dec, 2021. https://www.blueletterbible.org/lexicon/g3089/kjv/tr/0-1/.

Man has dominion on earth, and through Jesus Christ we bring down the kingdom reign of God.

I'll prove it some more:

> Jesus answered and said unto him, Verily, verily, I say unto thee, except a man be born again, he cannot see the kingdom of God. Nicodemus saith unto him, How can a man be born when he is old? Can he enter the second time into his mother's womb, and be born? Jesus answered, Verily, verily, I say unto thee, except a man be born of water and of the Spirit, he cannot enter into the kingdom of God. (John 3:3-5 KJV)

OK, so you must be born again to *see* the kingdom of God. You must be born of water and the Spirit to *enter* the kingdom of God. With words you establish the kingdom; with faith you enter. If only the salvation message of the kingdom has been revealed to you, do not leave it there. Now you can operate in the kingdom.

This is not talking about heaven. We are kingdom operators here on this side. Let God's kingdom reign on earth.

If you still don't get it, let me blow your mind—but since it's in the Bible, let's transform your mind.

> And be not conformed to this world: but be ye transformed by the renewing of your mind, that ye may prove what is that good, and acceptable, and perfect, will of God. (Romans 12:2 KJV)

The will of God is God's way of doing things, His system. That leads into establishing His kingdom on earth.

The Lord's Prayer says:

> Thy kingdom come. Thy will be done in earth, as it is in heaven. (Matthew 6:10 KJV)

So we're not in heaven; we are operating here on earth *as it is in heaven.*

Here's a question: Is there sickness and disease in heaven? Is there hate, discord, loneliness in heaven?

No, and there isn't in the kingdom either. Let the kingdom reign on earth *begin.* Amen. However, there is a god of this world and he has a system too. If you not operating in the kingdom of God, you are under the system of the little g.

> Satan, who is the god of this world, has blinded the minds of those who don't believe. They are unable to see the glorious light of the Good News. They don't understand this message about the

> glory of Christ, who is the exact likeness of God. (2 Corinthians 4:4 NLT)

So we have to disconnect from the little-g god of this world and connect to the kingdom of God in heaven and His way. We cannot operate with one foot in the kingdom of God and one foot in the world. That is called *religion*, my friends. Flee it.

Before Jesus was the Law, the old system, but we are in a new system, a new covenant, a better way, a New Testament.

> By so much was Jesus made a surety of a better testament. (Hebrews 7:22 KJV)

> But now hath he obtained a more excellent ministry, by how much also he is the mediator of a better covenant, which was established upon better promises. (Hebrews 8:6 KJV)

We are in relationship with God and walk in the Spirit of God, doing the will of God. This is operating in the kingdom of God.

Jesus said this:

> And saying, the time is fulfilled, and the kingdom of God is at hand: repent ye, and believe the gospel. (Mark 1:15 KJV)

What did He mean when He said that the kingdom of God was at hand? He meant it was now *available.*

Now, now is the time. Do not wait!

Jesus came to deliver the kingdom to us. The new way of doing things. Under grace, anointing, power, righteousness, and *glory!* Isaiah prophesied that when Jesus came He would bring a government. He would deliver to us a new system that we would now be operating in. It's not the world's way, the church's way, the American way, or the political way; it's the kingdom way or the highway. He came with the government upon His shoulder like a yoke that is easy. It's time to take off that heavy yoke, that beast of burden, and receive a Spirit-filled life with fullness of peace and joy.

> For unto us a child is born, unto us a son is given: and the government shall be upon his shoulder: and his name shall be called Wonderful, Counsellor, the mighty God, the everlasting Father, the Prince of Peace. Of the increase of his government and peace there shall be no end, upon the throne of David, and upon his kingdom, to order it, and to establish it with judgment and with justice from henceforth even for ever. The zeal of the Lord of hosts will perform this. (Isaiah 9:6-7 KJV)

Chapter 4: Kingdom Operators

The best and easiest way I can explain *operating* in God's kingdom is through the analogy of a themed amusement park. They are styled like small kingdoms. If someone gave you a free all-access pass to a park, all you would have to do is receive it. Think of it! They send you a wristband so you can move around as you please when you get there, and it is your favorite color. You park in the parking lot and walk to the turnstile and *you are in!* Access granted! But instead of going in, you decide to stand at the gate the whole day. You can see and hear everyone having the time of their lives, but you don't move. You have gained access, but did not enjoy what the kingdom had to offer. What a waste.

Your Father in heaven gave you the keys to His kingdom and an all-access pass too, and there are no shortcuts in the kingdom. Jesus says those who are last will be first and those who are first will be last. That is true, but the kingdom of God has divine acceleration! Are you kidding me? Fast pass included. Now that you have been standing at the gate, you have gained entry, but He wants to take you on a journey in which you will experience the greatest joy possible and new heights you have only dreamed of and didn't think were possible—rivers of living water, *dunamis power*. You have your ticket; you have gained entry. Now is the time to enjoy *all* the kingdom has to offer—with the Bible as your map and the Holy Spirit as your Guide.

> And this gospel of the kingdom will be preached in all the world as a witness to all the nations, and then the end will come. (Matthew 24:14)

Have we been preaching the wrong gospel? Scripture does not say the gospel of salvation will be preached in all the world. No, it says the *gospel of the kingdom* will be. The salvation message is the first step and entry point. Vital, but it's only the beginning. There is *more*. The kingdom is limitless. It does not have a one-day pass; it's eternal.

Jesus said unless you are born again, you cannot see the kingdom of God. Accepting Jesus is the gate. You are only born again once. You cannot be born again over and over. That's why Jesus compared it to your physical birth from your mother. This is what Jesus was explaining to Nicodemus in the book of John. The birth in the Spirit took place in the kingdom, so you are not of this world. You are a citizen of the kingdom now. You are on a special visa, operating in the kingdom.

There will come a time when that visa is up and you will go home. When you were born in the kingdom, you were born into His kingdom culture too. You talk differently, act differently, and respond differently than people in the world.

Additionally, when you are born again the Holy Spirit comes within you and makes His home in your heart. You can now literally "abide in Him" (John 15). The Holy Spirit brings with Him many gifts as well. They are different for everyone, but they include the gift of faith, healing, words of wisdom and knowledge, speaking in a heavenly language, and much, much more. He does not leave you unequipped for your calling. With Him as our Guide, we can enter the kingdom with one foot in front of the other. It's time we step into it confidently. You have been at the gate too long. Jesus paid too high of a price for you to stay at the gate your whole life. Your kingdom inheritance is available, but you have to *take* it.

> Jesus answered and said unto him, Verily, verily, I say unto thee, except a man be born again, he cannot see the kingdom of God. Nicodemus saith unto him, How can a man be born when he is old? can he enter the second time into his mother's womb, and be born? Jesus answered, Verily, verily, I say unto thee, except a man be born of water and of the Spirit,

> he cannot enter into the kingdom of God. (John 3:3-5 KJV)

So the fact is that we can operate in the kingdom of God on the earth. Can we also lose it? Can we step out of this kingdom operation? You better believe we can. We must be aware of this danger. Here's an example of a way we can step out of the kingdom.

> Then the disciples came to Jesus privately and said, "Why could we not cast it out?" So Jesus said to them, "Because of your unbelief; for assuredly, I say to you, if you have faith as a mustard seed, you will say to this mountain, 'Move from here to there,' and it will move; and nothing will be impossible for you. However, this kind does not go out except by prayer and fasting." (Matthew 17:19-21)

Unbelief is one way.

Let me tell you a story. There were three girls walking down a road: Catherine, Sarah, and Mary. They started discussing which one of them was the greatest of the group. And just like that, bam! They stepped out of the kingdom!

Comparison is a trap.

The disciples did it.

> Then a dispute arose among them as to which of them would be greatest. And Jesus, perceiving the thought of their heart, took a little child and set him by Him, and said to them, "Whoever receives this little child in My name receives Me; and whoever receives Me receives Him who sent Me. For he who is least among you all will be great." (Luke 9:46-48)

In His parables, Jesus taught us about how to stay in the kingdom and what could cause us to step out of it. It can happen moment to moment, but for Peter it happened verse to verse.

> And I also say to you that you are Peter, and on this rock I will build My church, and the gates of Hades shall not prevail against it. And I will give you the keys of the kingdom of heaven, and whatever you bind on earth will be bound in heaven, and **whatever you loose on earth will be loosed in heaven**. (Matthew 16:18-19, emphasis mine)

How wonderful. He is in the kingdom here, but then comes verse 23:

> Then Peter took Him aside and began to rebuke Him, saying, "Far be it from

> You, Lord; this shall not happen to You!" But He turned and said to Peter, "Get behind Me, Satan! You are an offense to Me, for you are not mindful of the things of God, but the things of men." (Matthew 16:22-23)

Three short verses later and Jesus says to Peter, "Get behind Me, Satan!" That sucks.

I know it's easier said than done, but we can't get hung up when we strike out because our next time at bat might be our homerun. The Enemy would love to keep us focused on our failures. Doing that prevents us from taking another turn at bat. But our heavenly Father wants us to focus on the possibility of the grand slam. He says we should pray big prayers and believe for big things. Jesus said greater are the things that you will do as you operate in the kingdom on earth. Greater! I'm shooting for greater.

> Most assuredly, I say to you, he who believes in Me, the works that I do he will do also; and greater works than these he will do, because I go to My Father. And whatever you ask in My name, that I will do, that the Father may be glorified in the Son. **If you ask anything in My name, I will do it**. (John 14:12-14, emphasis mine)

What a promise that is!

Jesus also said that if you build His kingdom on earth, He will usher in His kingdom reign on earth *as it is in heaven*.

Arguably there are different thoughts of what the greatest sermon of all time was. Many consider the Sermon on the Mount when Jesus spoke to the multitudes as His best. However, I prefer a time when He had an audience of one. That was the greatest sermon ever, and it's where we find the most quoted verse in the Bible—John 3:16.

> For God so loved the world that He gave His only begotten Son, that **whoever believes in Him should not perish but have everlasting life**. (John 3:16, emphasis mine)

Jesus said this during a secret nighttime meeting with Nicodemus, a Pharisee. There is something precious, one on one, that is missed in a crowd. The truth is that we don't need a crowd. We all have an audience of one every single day. Are we using those opportunities? You do not have to go to a developing nation to find someone who has never heard the good news. I asked my baker if she had heard the gospel and she had not. Our conversation was the first time she ever heard the good news of Jesus Christ. I had seen her often, but had not inquired until that day. How many people have we crossed paths with who are perishing, and we never asked them about it? Have you heard the good news?

Some people just don't know. We have a job to do. With each passing day, it is more important than ever. Don't get discouraged if you get rejected either. The Word went forth and will not return empty. Someone else will come after you and water it, and eventually it will bear fruit. It's all good.

It's time to tap into what's already inside you!

All over the earth, there is oil and gold, just waiting to be tapped. We have this hidden treasure in earthen vessels. I'm writing to say that I see the gold inside of you and to call it out. Perhaps you've come to the kingdom *for such a time as this.*

> But we have this treasure in earthen vessels, that the excellency of the power may be of God, and not of us. (2 Corinthians 4:7 KJV)

Chapter 5: Kingdom Moves

What are *kingdom moves?* I will list them just as Jesus did: casting out demons, speaking in tongues, taking up serpents, not being poisoned, laying hands on the sick.

> And these signs will follow those who believe: In My name they will cast out demons; they will speak with new tongues; they will take up serpents; and if they drink anything deadly, it will by no means hurt them; they will lay hands on the sick, and they will recover. (Mark 16:17-18)

Wow! Casting out demons and speaking in a heavenly language that the Enemy can't understand? Healing people? Even so, it's the taking up of serpents and drinking poison that's got me scratching my head a little. I know there are churches that actually handle snakes on Sundays to see if they get poisoned. I think that's weird, especially since Jesus answered Satan when he was tempting Him with these words:

> And Jesus answered and said to him, "It has been said, 'You shall not tempt the Lord your God.'" (Luke 4:12)

This means that these gifts are given as needed. We're not supposed to "play" with snakes. No foolish tests involved. I want to make kingdom moves, but we can skip the whole snake handling and drinking poison part.

But what does this mean? I've learned if I ask God, He will answer. So I looked this up in *Strong's Exhaustive Concordance*, and the snakes used in this verse refer to a "figurative" snake "(a type of sly cunning)" and "an artful, malicious person, especially Satan."[3] The poison in that verse is described as "deadly." According to Strong's, this word refers to something that is "poisonous, fatal."[4]

As we make kingdom moves, we will encounter snakes—figurative ones—cunning and malicious people who mean to do us harm. However, God guarantees that they will not poison our souls or damage our eternal life in any way. God's got us. Wow! That's a horse of a different color.

3. "G3789 - ophis - Strong's Greek Lexicon (kjv)." Blue Letter Bible. Accessed 1 Dec, 2021. https://www.blueletterbible.org/lexicon/g3789/kjv/tr/0-1/.

4. "G2286 - thanasimos - Strong's Greek Lexicon (kjv)." Blue Letter Bible. Accessed 1 Dec, 2021. https://www.blueletterbible.org/lexicon/g2286/kjv/tr/0-1/.

Jesus told us about them so we would be aware and even expect them. We are not to be afraid of these "snakes" because we have been sealed in Christ's blood—signed, sealed, and delivered!

> In Him you also trusted, after you heard the word of truth, the gospel of your salvation; in whom also, having believed, you were sealed with the Holy Spirit of promise, who is the guarantee of our inheritance until the redemption of the purchased possession, to the praise of His glory. (Ephesians 1:13-14)

So don't be afraid to make kingdom moves. Make *big* moves. Go *big* or go home. Big moves are kingdom moves. What are you afraid of? Jesus has *all* authority on earth, under the earth, and above the earth. He is all-powerful. He took everything back at the cross when He took the keys to death, hell, and the grave. He has *now* given us the keys to the kingdom too. What do keys do? They lock and unlock doors, which means nothing shall block you anymore.

But that's not all; there's more! The Lord will work with you, confirming His Word with accompanying signs!

> So then, after the Lord had spoken to them, He was received up into heaven, and sat down at the right hand of God. And they

> went out and preached everywhere, the Lord working with them and confirming the word through the accompanying signs. Amen. (Mark 16:19-20)

The signs He is talking about glorify God and let people know that He loves them.

We follow signs every day, so don't be surprised when signs and wonders follow you now. They should.

Chapter 6: Dear Supervising Fruit Inspector

If you are in a relationship or friendship that is not producing good fruit, you need to cut off that branch. We all recognize the danger of hanging out with those who are toxic to us.

Healthy fruit feeds your soul and brings life, while rotten fruit will make you sick. Similarly, relationships feed your soul one way or the other. They are healthy or poisonous, growing or toxic. There is no in-between. It's one or the other. You are either cultivating blessings or curses.

> But the fruit of the Spirit is love, joy, peace, longsuffering, kindness, goodness, faithfulness, gentleness, self-control. Against such there is no law. (Galatians 5:22-23)

If you are not producing healthy fruit, you may be producing poisonous fruit. Those who produce the works of the flesh will not inherit the kingdom of God. Spiritual death is at their door.

> Now the works of the flesh are evident, which are: adultery, fornication, uncleanness, lewdness, idolatry, sorcery, hatred, contentions, jealousies, outbursts of wrath, selfish ambitions, dissensions, heresies, envy, murders, drunkenness, revelries, and the like; of which I tell you beforehand, just as I also told you in time past, that those who practice such things will not inherit the kingdom of God. (Galatians 5:19-21)

A life producing the works of the flesh is not balanced and is marked by laziness, hatred, strife, bitterness, and neglect.

Be careful with whom you are connected. Together you will either produce good fruit that nourishes others or toxins that bring sickness and kill. We cannot blame those with whom we have allowed ourselves to make alliances either. A dry season can only excuse a lack of fruit for a short time. Eventually the farmers have to take responsibility for losing their green thumb.

While cultivating good fruit, we must maintain healthy boundaries. This is true in any garden. Wildlife and the elements pose dual threats to a carefully cultivated garden. Fencing provides a barrier between those threats and your fruit. The local animal population enjoys munching on your tender fruit. Beware of them! They spoil the vine. Our boundaries keep out the foxes while preventing them from feasting on the fruit of our labor.

> Catch us the foxes, the little foxes that spoil the vines, for our vines have tender grapes. (Song of Solomon 2:15)

Over the years, I have seen this truth used out of context. This verse does not mean we only have people around us who are good fruit producers, because we are called to minister to a lost, hurting, and dying world. It simply means we are not *connected,* or in covenant, with those who produce bad fruit until they produce life-giving fruit. Christians have used this verse as an excuse to not be Christlike too. I have heard many "professional fruit inspectors" talk more about the rotten fruit they see around them rather than the production of good fruit. (Maybe *they* are the problem.) If you think you are called to be a supervising fruit inspector, you should know that it is *not* a ministry.

The Bible says we will know them by their fruit—not we will judge them by their fruit. Let's feed those around us with good fruit that brings life. They've already tasted the poisonous kind that made them sick! Psalm 34 says that we should "taste and see the Lord is good" (Psalm 34:8). There is a saying if you never tasted a bad apple you would not appreciate a good one.

Unfortunately, there are people who have never tasted a good apple. In that, the church has got it wrong.

The fruit of the Holy Spirit is healthy and beneficial to you and everyone around you. It feeds and nourishes. What does it take to make fruit? Just a seed.

> Having been born again, not of corruptible seed but incorruptible, through the word of God which lives and abides forever. (1 Peter 1:23)

When you were born again, you were produced by God's seed, which is incorruptible. God's seed produces *God* inside you. As we went over in the last chapter, God sowed His Spirit inside you. Naturally, the fruit of the Spirit follows, bringing life all around you. Remember love is the first fruit. This is the *agape* love of God. *Agape* love is like the peel of the orange. It envelops the slices or sections within the orange. Those slices are love, joy, peace, long-suffering, kindness, goodness, faithfulness, gentleness, self-control. All of God's fruit stems from love. We are to do all things in *love.* As we do this, we give the first fruits unto God as His saints.

> Let all that you do be done with love. I urge you, brethren—you know the household of Stephanas, that it is the firstfruits of Achaia, and that they have

devoted themselves to the ministry of the saints. (1 Corinthians 16:14-15)

Chapter 7: Glory to Glory

The Father's heart is that you grow from glory to glory. I'm going to be honest—I don't always feel glorious. That is why we cannot always trust our feelings. They can deceive us. Against popular belief, this has nothing to do with momentary circumstances. The fact that you are being transformed from one degree of glory to another does not mean you will not have trials. It means that as we repent and continually seek the Lord's face, He will continually be revealed to us more deeply, transforming us into His image, like a mirror.

> But we all, with open face beholding as in a glass the glory of the Lord, are changed into the same image from glory to glory, even as by the Spirit of the Lord. (2 Corinthians 3:18 KJV)

> For our light affliction, which is but for a moment, worketh for us a far more

> exceeding and eternal weight of glory.
> (2 Corinthians 4:17 KJV)

Second Corinthians 4:17 is one of my favorite promises. The things we go through don't seem like "light afflictions" while we are experiencing them. However, this verse illuminates the truth that our trials cannot even be compared to the glory that will be revealed. No comparison! God's glory far outweighs it. The glory revealed in us (and through us) creates a deeper and stronger anointing. When you have received Jesus Christ, the Anointed One, you now carry the anointing too. You are anointed! Say that out loud: "*I am anointed.*" We all want a deeper and stronger anointing. We may sometimes look at brothers and sisters in Christ and think that we want their anointing, but the truth is that they had to go through something to receive that level. We all want it, but do we want to go through what they went through? In truth, we all have a special anointing that we carry, usually birthed from what we have been through. For instance, if you have been a victim of abuse, you are anointed to minister to those who have suffered the same thing, bringing healing to them. In the same vein, if you have been healed of a life-threatening disease, you are anointed to minister in great faith for healing for others.

In the Old Testament, God gave Moses clear instructions on how to make the anointing oil used in the temple. We are going to break it down now.

> Take thou also unto thee principal spices, of pure myrrh five hundred shekels, and of sweet cinnamon half so much, even two hundred and fifty shekels, and of sweet calamus two hundred and fifty shekels, and of cassia five hundred shekels, after the shekel of the sanctuary, and of oil olive an hin: and thou shalt make it an oil of holy ointment, an ointment compound after the art of the apothecary: it shall be an holy anointing oil. (Exodus 30:23-25 KJV)

God is telling Moses to measure out these four spices in olive oil. It was used to anoint everything in the tabernacle, where the presence of the Lord would dwell as well as on the priests. We are under the New Testament today, which means *we are the tabernacle* now. *We* are where the presence of the Lord dwells today. We are a royal priesthood. This compound was put together like a medicine. This is the anointing we carry. The olive oil is a type of the Holy Spirit, and it is noteworthy that these four spices had to be submerged into the Holy Spirit.

Ingredient 1: Myrrh

Myrrh is the "yellowish-brown to reddish-brown aromatic gum resin with a bitter slightly pungent taste obtained from a tree (especially Commiphora abyssinica of the family Burseraceae) of eastern Africa and Arabia."[5] Myrrh is a stunted shrub that has been used medicinally for centuries, from which a sweet-smelling gum resin pours out like teardrops.[6] This is the natural pouring out of the plant. Myrrh can also be obtained by cutting the bark. In our lives, this reflects a wound or trauma. Myrrh flows from the things that happen in our life; circumstances happen and the myrrh is poured out. The teardrop that comes out of the plant is broken off, ground into a powder, and mixed into the oil. This is a process, and the process becomes part of our anointing. Myrrh is very fragrant, which denotes the sweet smell of sacrifice to the Lord.

Ingredient 2: Cinnamon

Cinnamon is "the aromatic, dried bark of any of several tropical trees (genus Cinnamomum) yielding a culinary spice, oil, and flavoring, especially a small roll or quill of cinnamon bark," or a "tan to dark brown spice that is prepared from cinnamon bark by powdering and has a somewhat sweet and spicy taste."[7] Rarer then myrrh, the cinnamon tree has stiff green leaves. To get to the cinnamon, "the outside bark is scraped off the branches are then ripped up lengthways with a knife, and the inner bark is gradually loosened, till it can be entirely taken. Exposure to the sun causes it to curl up.

5. "Myrrh," Merriam-Webster (Merriam-Webster), accessed October 15, 2021, https://www.merriam-webster.com/dictionary/myrrh.

6. "Myrrh," NETBible: Myrrh, accessed October 15, 2021, http://classic.net.bible.org/dictionary.php?word=myrrh.

7. "Cinnamon," Merriam-Webster (Merriam-Webster), accessed October 15, 2021, https://www.merriam-webster.com/dictionary/cinnamon.

The pieces of bark so curled are called quills."[8] In our lives, God will peel the layers back and scrape us to get to the good that is within. After this process, cinnamon is shelved until it is ground again. Many of us can relate to this "shelf life" period of time. Sometimes cinnamon quills are pulled back, scraped, and then put in a pot to boil. This heating process is like a "refiner's fire" and separates the inner rind from the outer bark.[9] As we yield to His fire, He brings us to maturity so others can see God within us. However, this requires removing the coarse outer shell and peeling our masks off.

Ingredient 3: Calamus

Calamus, or sweet flag, is "the aromatic peeled and dried rhizome of the sweet flag that is the source of a carcinogenic essential oil," and the "the hollow basal portion of a feather below the vane."[10] Also known as sugar cane stalks, this rare plant is unusually sweet and fragrant, especially when it's bruised. When calamus is broken, a sweet fragrance is released. We can either allow our brokenness to be processed by the Holy Spirit or not. If we allow Him to minister to us, we will release this same sweet scent, the aroma of Christ. This sweet fragrance will attract people and draw people to Jesus.

8. Elizabeth Mayo, "Lessons on Objects PDF," PDF, n.d., accessed October 15, 2021.

9. "Cinnamon," NETBible: Cinnamon, accessed October 15, 2021, http://classic.net.bible.org/dictionary.php?word=Cinnamon.

10. "Calamus," Merriam-Webster (Merriam-Webster), accessed October 15, 2021, https://www.merriam-webster.com/dictionary/calamus.

When this reed is crushed, broken, and processed, it becomes a part of the anointing in our life.

Ingredient 4: Cassia

Cassia, or less commonly cassia cinnamon, is "the dried, aromatic bark of several tropical trees (genus Cinnamomum) that yields a reddish brown to dark brown spice sold as and used similarly to true cinnamon but having a usually stronger, more spicy character," and also refers to "the powdered spice produced from cassia bark" or "any of a genus (Cassia) of leguminous herbs, shrubs, and trees of warm regions."[11] Cassia has been used by doctors as a purging medicine. There will be things that must be removed from our life too. In the natural, we often want to hang on to habits and thinking that need to be purged from us. As we allow the Holy Spirit to take them from us, this becomes part of our anointing too. Sometimes it's sin, bad habits, lies we believe, or even people who need to be removed from our life. The word *purge* means "to clear of guilt, to make free of something unwanted, and to get rid of."[12] Like cinnamon, cassia is gathered from the inner bark. Peeling us wide open, God wants access to our inner selves.

---

11. "Cassia," Merriam-Webster (Merriam-Webster), accessed October 15, 2021, https://www.merriam-webster.com/dictionary/cassia.

12. "Purge," Merriam-Webster (Merriam-Webster), accessed October 15, 2021, https://www.merriam-webster.com/dictionary/purge.

After Moses put together these four ingredients, then they were blended into the olive oil (the Holy Spirit). They were mixed up together. We must let the Holy Spirit blend the important circumstances in our lives. You will notice a settling that develops if you don't keep the oil moving. You have to keep the oil moving!

Stir up the gifts placed within you by your Father. Growing from glory to glory refers to going from the presence of God to the presence of God.

How do I tell if the anointing is off? That's easy. It smells funny.

> But I have all, and abound: I am full, having received of Epaphroditus the things which were sent from you, an odour of a sweet smell, a sacrifice acceptable, wellpleasing to God. But my God shall supply all your need according to his riches in glory by Christ Jesus. Now unto God and our Father be glory for ever and ever. Amen. (Philippians 4:18-20 KJV)

When they anointed the priests, the oil was poured out—not just a little on their fingertips. No. This oil was poured over their heads. It was messy.

> It is like the precious oil upon the head, running down on the beard, the beard of

> Aaron, running down on the edge of his garments. (Psalm 133:2)

They poured the oil on the head, but in this description in Psalms of when Moses anointed Aaron, the oil ran down his garments into his beard and on down, covering his whole body. Where did the oil end up? On the floor! The glory is on the floor. When we humble ourselves before the Lord, His glory is revealed in and through us. In Genesis, when the Lord is establishing His covenant with Abram, He tells him to walk blamelessly. But Abram took a different position. Let's take a look:

> When Abram was ninety-nine years old, the Lord appeared to Abram and said to him, "I am Almighty God; walk before Me and be blameless. And I will make My covenant between Me and you, and will multiply you exceedingly." Then Abram fell on his face, and God talked with him, saying: "As for Me, behold, My covenant is with you, and you shall be a father of many nations. No longer shall your name be called Abram, but your name shall be Abraham; for I have made you a father of many nations." (Genesis 17:1-5)

Abram fell on his face in reverence and worship. Taking this position gave him a name change and his covenant with God was established.

Chapter 7: Glory to Glory

There are several places in which the glory of the Lord was revealed when God's worshipers hit the floor:

> So Moses and Aaron went from the presence of the assembly to the door of the tabernacle of meeting, and they fell on their faces. And the glory of the Lord appeared to them. (Numbers 20:6)

> And Moses and Aaron went into the tabernacle of meeting, and came out and blessed the people. Then the glory of the Lord appeared to all the people, and fire came out from before the Lord and consumed the burnt offering and the fat on the altar. When all the people saw it, they shouted and fell on their face. (Leviticus 9:23-24)

> Now when all the people saw it, they fell on their faces; and they said, "The Lord, He is God! The Lord, He is God!" (1 Kings 18:39)

These are just few of many examples. In the New Testament, when the wise men encountered the Lord, they also fell down in worship. Pay attention to the gifts they brought, and look for the familiar ingredients we just studied that were in the anointing oil.

> And when they had come into the house, they saw the young Child with Mary His mother, and fell down and worshiped Him. And when they had opened their treasures, they presented gifts to Him: gold, frankincense, and myrrh. (Matthew 2:11)

In the throne room of grace in Revelation, the angels and the elders are on their faces in reverence. This is the posture of worship.

> All the angels stood around the throne and the elders and the four living creatures, and fell on their faces before the throne and worshiped God. (Revelation 7:11)

Again I say, the glory is on the floor!

Warriors of faith, understand this: *Victory* starts on the floor.

In Scripture, there is a story of a warrior who understood this principle. She was a woman with an "issue"—in her case an issue of blood. We *all* have issues—physical or spiritual. We all deal with something every single day. This woman was very smart because she knew who to go to. Our choice about where we run to deal with our issues has the potential to heal or destroy us. We can run to drugs, alcohol, or even other unhealthy people with issues, to mask the pain of our own issues. Misery loves company. These options are only temporary Band-Aids that leave us wanting more, and they will take from us until there is nothing left. There is a better way—the best way. Jesus is the way, the truth, and the life. Go to Him, even if you feel so beaten down that you are crawling. If you are at such a low point, you are the in the perfect position for victory. This woman had spent all she had to be healed, but one touch from the hem of Jesus' garment was what she needed. She was instantly restored. This required her to *stretch.* You too, may have to stretch your faith to receive the glory and take it. Yes, I meant to say "take it." This woman did not ask before she touched Jesus. Jesus didn't even know who had touched Him. The disciples were confused because a crowd surrounded Jesus, meaning everyone was touching Him. But this touch was different. This touch He felt. Not much was different back then than it is today. Jesus was surrounded by a multitude of clout chasers. In a world of clout chasers be a kingdom chaser—the one who pushes through, knowing where their help comes from, and takes it. I want to be the one Jesus *feels*. Jesus asked who had touched Him because He felt the power going out. Here's the story:

> Now a woman, having a flow of blood for twelve years, who had spent all her livelihood on physicians and could not be healed by any, came from behind and touched the border of His garment. And immediately her flow of blood stopped.

And Jesus said, "Who touched Me?" When all denied it, Peter and those with him said, "Master, the multitudes throng and press You, and You say, 'Who touched Me?'" But Jesus said, "Somebody touched Me, for I perceived power going out from Me." Now when the woman saw that she was not hidden, she came trembling; and falling down before Him, she declared to Him in the presence of all the people the reason she had touched Him and how she was healed immediately. And He said to her, "Daughter, be of good cheer; your faith has made you well. Go in peace." (Luke 8:43-48)

Chapter 8: Levels

> And He Himself gave some to be apostles, some prophets, some evangelists, and some pastors and teachers, for the equipping of the saints for the work of ministry, for the edifying of the body of Christ. (Ephesians 4:11-12)

You are a piece of the equipment, a part of the puzzle depicting the big picture that only God knows. The first of these gifts God gave us is the office of apostle.

> Truly the signs of an apostle were accomplished among you with all perseverance, in signs and wonders and mighty deeds. (2 Corinthians 12:12)

The fruit of perseverance is the first sign of an apostle. This word *perseverance* here in the Greek is *hupomeno*. It is a compound of the words *hupo* and *meno*. *Hupo* means "under" and *meno* means "to abide or endure."[13] When the two words are put together, it describes a person who "is unswerved from his deliberate purpose and his loyalty to faith and piety by even the greatest trials and sufferings" because he or she is committed to the task.[14]

This word has been translated as endurance and staying power. My favorite translation is hang-in-there power. Some read this verse with a focus on signs and wonders and mighty deeds, and they skip the perseverance, but perseverance is the very first word used. In my opinion, it's the greatest miracle of all, and that is why it is mentioned first. It's a supernatural perseverance. A supernatural grace, a divine favor.

Signs and wonders can come and go, but this is sign that remains. It is just as real as any miracle or mighty deed. Perseverance empowers us beyond our natural strength.

The apostle is only the first gift God gave His body. He also gave us prophets, evangelists, pastors, and teachers. All of them are supposed to work together to equip everyone so they can fulfil the ministry God has apportioned for each person in the entire body of Christ. We are all supposed to serve one another.

Whatever our place in the body, every one of us has to go through the same stages of growth. We *all* have a

13. "G5281 - hypomonē - Strong's Greek Lexicon (kjv)." Blue Letter Bible. Accessed 1 Dec, 2021. https://www.blueletterbible.org/lexicon/g5281/kjv/tr/0-1/.

14. Ibid.

position, a part to play, and a duty to equip the saints for the work of the ministry and to edify the body of Christ.

There are levels of spiritual maturity just like in our physical life. We are born as a baby, and when we are birthed in the Spirit it is the same. In this chapter, we will go over the levels in the Spirit and the needs and dangers involved so we can better understand the importance of growth. It is imperative to remember that whatever level we are on, we are fighting the same Devil. We must be aware of his schemes and the tricks he uses. We are destroyed by lack of knowledge, but with the understanding of the truth we are set free and overcome every tactic of our adversary.

This chart outlines each level.

Spiritual Maturity	Greek	Scripture	Need	Danger
Baby	*brephos* (infant)	1 John 2:12	Assurance	Doubt
Toddler	*nepios* (without speech)	Ephesians 4:14	Discernment	Easily led astray
Child	*paidia* (evil, 3 to 12 years)	Hebrew 12:5	Discipline	Rebellion
Teenager	*neaniskoi* (full of energy)	1 John 2:13	Victory	Frustration
Father	*pater* (Father)	1 Corinthians 4:14	Reproduce	Apathy (don't care)

> Jesus answered and said to him, "Most assuredly, I say to you, unless one is born again, he cannot see the kingdom of God." (John 3:3)

> Jesus answered, "Most assuredly, I say to you, unless one is born of water and the Spirit, he cannot enter the kingdom of God. That which is born of the flesh is flesh, and that which is born of the Spirit is spirit." (John 3:5-6)

The new birth is from the Spirit of God. Salvation does not make bad people good; it makes dead people *alive!*

The first stage level in life and in the Spirit is the baby. Baby in the Greek is the word *brephos* or "baby."[15] A baby has no past; they are innocent. Babies are easily frustrated, disturbed, upset, and hurt. Sound familiar? A baby needs assurance.

> As newborn babes, desire the pure milk of the word, that you may grow thereby. (1 Peter 2:2)

The danger for a baby believer is doubt. They need constant assurance by the body of Christ in love.

---

15. "G1025 - brephos - Strong's Greek Lexicon (kjv)." Blue Letter Bible. Accessed 1 Dec, 2021. https://www.blueletterbible.org/lexicon/g1025/kjv/tr/0-1/.

> I write to you, little children, because your sins are forgiven you for His name's sake. (1 John 2:12)

> Whoever has been born of God does not sin, for His seed remains in him; and he cannot sin, because he has been born of God. (1 John 3:9)

If you have been born of God, His seed remains in you. The word "seed" used here is the Greek word *sperma*, and it is where we get the scientific word sperm. In the same way your natural father birthed you, you are God's divine seed and have His DNA.[16]

As the body of Christ, we cannot abort our baby believers through our own selfishness and laziness. Have we become so involved with our own ministries or "careers" that we have lost what ministry is about? Our babies need the spiritually mature to feed, hold, and guide them. Parents have a natural reaction and human instinct to protect their offspring from harm. In the spirit, we should have the same instinct over our baby believers. They are at risk too. They depend on us for everything to survive, so we must keep a watchful eye and stand guard.

We have lost too many babies in the church to spiritual abortion. It has become an epidemic. We cannot

16. "G4690 - sperma - Strong's Greek Lexicon (kjv)." Blue Letter Bible. Accessed 1 Dec, 2021. https://www.blueletterbible.org/lexicon/g4690/kjv/tr/0-1/.

birth and leave them. The Enemy comes immediately to pluck the seed whenever he can. He has been after the seed from the beginning in the garden; that is why there is enmity between the woman (or womb-man) and the serpent.

> And I will put enmity between you and the woman, and between your seed and her Seed; He shall bruise your head, and you shall bruise His heel. (Genesis 3:15)

The next level is the toddler. A toddler is a child approximately twelve to thirty-six months old. The word *toddler* is derived from "to toddle," which means to walk unsteadily. In Greek, it is referred to by the word *nepios*, meaning "unlearned and unenlightened."[17] Toddlers don't know a lot yet. This is obvious by their speech. Everything is pretty new to them, especially the things of the kingdom. In his assault against the kingdom, the Enemy has placed traps for the growing Christian child of which we need to be aware.

> That we should no longer be children, tossed to and fro and carried about with every wind of doctrine, by the trickery of men, in the cunning craftiness of deceitful plotting. (Ephesians 4:14)

---

17. "G3516 - nēpios - Strong's Greek Lexicon (kjv)." Blue Letter Bible. Accessed 1 Dec, 2021. https://www.blueletterbible.org/lexicon/g3516/kjv/tr/0-1/.

Toddlers are in need of discernment or they will be easily lead astray. False doctrines, religious spirits, and cults like Christian Science, Jehovah's Witnesses, and the New Age movement, amongst others, want to get a hold of them, and bam! They are in bondage again. They are innocent and unaware of the dangers. In this naïve state, they can easily be led astray as the Bible says by "every wind of doctrine," meaning they are so unsteady in their walk that someone could blow on them and they would fall down. Picture a toddler walking along the coffee table. When they first let go and try to walk, they always fall after only a couple of steps. Just as parents hold a toddler's hands so they can learn to walk, mentors do the same with spiritual toddlers. Doctrines can be dangerous to the immature. They are in desperate need of fathers who will rise up and protect and mentor them in all truth. I read a shocking statistic that said that more than 80 percent of pastors who have graduated from Bible school leave the ministry within just five years.[18] They have a lot of trouble because they are on their own. If this is happening to seminary graduates, I can only imagine how the young and lonely Christian is faring.

What about the person who "gets saved" at an evangelistic crusade? Here's some information on that: "In a 1990 interview with PBS, Billy Graham himself stated his belief that only about 25% of those who come for-

18. Daniel Venturino, Godly culture, February 27, 2015, https://godlyculture.com/guess-what-%80-of-seminary-andor-bible-college-graduates-leave-in-less-than-5-years-the-ministry/.

ward at one of his events actually became Christians. In recent years, studies have shown that only 6% of people who 'come forward' at an evangelistic crusade are any different in their beliefs or behavior one year later."[19] Of course, it is "estimated that Billy Graham preached to more than 200 million people, and 6% of 200 million is still 12 million. That's significant."[20] I would never want to diminish Mr. Graham's achievement at all. I just want to point out that we are not doing especially well in the retention department. This needs to change, but it is up the church to rise up.

> My people are destroyed for lack of knowledge. (Hosea 4:6a)

> Wisdom and knowledge will be the stability of your times, and the strength of salvation; the fear of the Lord is His treasure. (Isaiah 33:6)

Wisdom and knowledge will be the stability of your times. A toddler's walk is unsteady, but wisdom and knowledge will be the stability they need. Wisdom comes when knowledge is correctly applied. The wise build upon the rock. We must build ourselves upon the Word of God.

---

19. Jeremy Myers, "Is Crusade Evangelism Effective?," Redeeming God, June 1, 2013, https://redeeminggod.com/crusade-evangelism-effective/.

20. Ibid.

> Happy is the man who finds wisdom, and the man who gains understanding. (Proverbs 3:13)

Finders, keepers!

The next level is the child, which means to be "immature or a child in training."[21] Children are in desperate need of discipline or they will rebel. Listen to me closely—teenagers do not rebel. Younger *undisciplined* children are the ones who rebel. We see it continue in teenagers because it is not properly dealt with at this level.

> And you have forgotten the exhortation which speaks to you as to sons: "My son, do not despise the chastening of the Lord, nor be discouraged when you are rebuked by Him; for whom the Lord loves He chastens, and scourges every son whom He receives." If you endure chastening, God deals with you as with sons; for what son is there whom a father does not chasten? But if you are without chastening, of which all have become partakers, then you are illegitimate and not sons. Furthermore, we have had human fathers who corrected us, and we paid them respect. Shall we not much

21. "G3813 - paidion - Strong's Greek Lexicon (kjv)." Blue Letter Bible. Accessed 1 Dec, 2021. https://www.blueletterbible.org/lexicon/g3813/kjv/tr/0-1/.

> more readily be in subjection to the Father of spirits and live? For they indeed for a few days chastened us as seemed best to them, but He for our profit, that we may be partakers of His holiness. Now no chastening seems to be joyful for the present, but painful; nevertheless, afterward it yields the peaceable fruit of righteousness to those who have been trained by it. (Hebrews 12:5-11)

The Greek word used in this passage in verse 5 for "child" is *paideia* and specifically refers to "the whole training and education of children (which relates to the cultivation of mind and morals, and employs for this purpose now commands and admonitions, now reproof and punishment). It also includes the training and care of the body" and "instruction which aims at increasing virtue and chastisement, chastening (of the evils with which God visits men for their amendment)."[22] Note the use of the words "chastisement and chastening." This stage is crucial to developing a spiritually mature believer.

The "don't do as I do, but do as I say" mentality will not work. We must model a real Christian walk before them. If you correct the child about something you still practice yourself, you are teaching them a double standard. You have become no better than a Pharisee—a

22. "G3809 - paideia - Strong's Greek Lexicon (kjv)." Blue Letter Bible. Accessed 1 Dec, 2021. https://www.blueletterbible.org/lexicon/g3809/kjv/tr/0-1/.

Pharisee Parent. The Pharisee Parent is a big problem in the kingdom.

Children form their conscience by what they have seen. Every single individual has a different conscience according to how they were raised. So someone may feel that certain practices are immoral, while someone else may not feel those same things are bad. This speaks of the conscience, not the Holy Spirit; they are *totally* different. We all have a differently formed conscience, but there's only one Holy Spirit. He is the one true Guide into all truth. No matter how you were raised and what you are coming out of, we have hope in Christ Jesus and the power to overcome by the blood of the Lamb with a built-in best Friend, the gift of the Holy Spirit, our Helper and Guide for the journey.

The next level is the teenager and is aptly described by the Greek word *neamiskoi*, which means "young man."[23] As this verse demonstrates, young men are overcomers. They are exuberant and strong.

> I write to you, young men, because you have overcome the wicked one. (1 John 2:13b)

The teenager is in need of victory or they will be in danger of frustration. Teenagers are so full of energy that if they don't get victory right away, they become discouraged. That zeal they once had is quickly deflat-

23. "G3495 - neaniskos - Strong's Greek Lexicon (kjv)." Blue Letter Bible. Accessed 1 Dec, 2021. https://www.blueletterbible.org/lexicon/g3495/kjv/tr/0-1/.

ed. He or she will start to think: *This doesn't work for me. Everything I do fails. I am never going to get a victory.* Lie after lie after lie.

If you need advice or a job done, call a teenager. They already know it all. They've got life figured out and haven't even paid a cell phone bill! I know this because I was once a teenager. I didn't realize until I raised one of my own how significant a victory in their life was. If they do not have a sense of overcoming, their frustration will cause them to have an "I don't care" mentality, while in reality *they care very much.*

Teenagers will do anything they want. Try to get them to do something you want them to do. I have learned from experience to lead by example. It is the best approach. You won't know if it is truly working though, so prepare for that. Teenagers will not tell you what they really think deep down more often than not. You may even think that nothing is getting through. This is a lie. It is working! Sometimes you will not see or know how much you are getting through for a long time, but spiritual mothers and fathers are essential to raising a healthy teenager in the Spirit. They take everything in like a sponge. When you may not be there—when they are squeezed, what they have been taught will come out. This rule works on both sides of the spectrum—good or bad. Our teenagers need spiritual mentors to rise up and take them under their wings. That brings us to the final level of spiritual maturity.

> For though you might have ten thousand instructors in Christ, yet you do not have many fathers; for in Christ Jesus I have begotten you through the gospel. (1 Corinthians 4:15)

The Greek word *pater*—which can be a "father, (heavenly) Father, ancestor, elder, senior" or "one who imparts life and is committed to it"—is used here.[24]

Fathers don't preach sermons; they *demonstrate* them.

Fathers in the body of Christ are not just male; they are female too. They are the highest level of spiritual maturity. Fathers need to reproduce themselves. Their danger is a state of apathy in which they no longer care if they are not successful in this. The day you cross over from childhood to adolescence to adulthood is the day you take responsibility for others. Fathers are the highest level of spiritual maturity because they choose this responsibility. Fathers are full of knowledge and wisdom. Because of their life experience, others can glean from them. *Father* is a title of honor, and fathers should be treated with respect. They protect and take charge of those around them. Speaking the truth in love, they emulate the heart of our Father in heaven. They take His instructions to go into the world and make disciples seriously.

24. "G3962 - patēr - Strong's Greek Lexicon (kjv)." Blue Letter Bible. Accessed 1 Dec, 2021. https://www.blueletterbible.org/lexicon/g3962/kjv/tr/0-1/.

> "Go therefore and make disciples of all the nations, baptizing them in the name of the Father and of the Son and of the Holy Spirit, teaching them to observe all things that I have commanded you; and lo, I am with you always, even to the end of the age." Amen. (Matthew 28:19-20)

Even though a father is the highest level of spiritual maturity, being one does not mean you have arrived. There is *always* more to learn in the kingdom and the King *never* runs out of revelation. An unteachable spirit cannot be used by our Father God anymore. We should always be growing and moving forward, or we are in danger of going backward. This can happen. We can go back to a different stage, so it is imperative that we have an understanding of the levels of spiritual maturity so we can prevent this.

The level you yield to the Holy Spirit is the level of transformation into the very image of Christ that you reach. The level in which you seek Christ face to face is the level He will manifest Himself to you! In His presence is where transformation takes place. It is where you *level up*.

This growth from level to level is a lifelong process. As we walk in obedience, we will grow according to His will.

He who has My commandments and keeps them, it is he who loves Me. And he who loves Me will be loved by My Father, and I will love him and manifest Myself to him. (John 14:21)

Chapter 9: Prepare for War!

I have written eight chapters in order to get to this one. And this one is different as it is more of a prophetic encouragement than it is a teaching.

Let's start in the book of Joel. Joel is only three chapters long. Short but mighty. I can relate; I'm short too. It is not always quantity but quality. In Hebrew, the name *Joel* means "Yahweh is God."[25]

Joel's message started with repentance and the coming of the day of the Lord. Repent and believe! Sound familiar?

Jesus' message was the same.

> From that time Jesus began to preach and to say, "Repent, for the kingdom of heaven is at hand." (Matthew 4:17)

25. Mike Campbell, "Meaning, Origin and History of the Name Joel," Behind the Name, accessed October 20, 2021, https://www.behindthename.com/name/joel.

> Alas for the day! For the day of the Lord is at hand; it shall come as destruction from the Almighty. (Joel 1:15)

The kingdom is at hand, and a mighty army needs to protect and serve the King. Joel, in his prophetic ministry, saw an army of *warriors* called to defend the King of Kings and His kingdom—the kingdom the Son of Man would deliver in the end. Joel's word was delivered to the tribe of Judah, but also speaks of the nation as a whole. Joel says:

> So rend your heart, and not your garments; return to the Lord your God, for He is gracious and merciful, slow to anger, and of great kindness; and He relents from doing harm. (Joel 2:13)

God has been after His people's hearts from the beginning. Nothing we can do makes us worthy. Tearing our clothes and rolling around on the ground in the dirt will not move the heart of God. That is like a child having a tantrum. It is your heart that moves toward God, and moves His heart toward you. We must turn to the Lord our God. Repentance means to turn around and go another way. This could be as simple as changing your mind. This promise in James sums it up:

> Draw near to God and He will draw near to you. (James 4:8a)

In Joel 2:28-32, God gave us the promise of His Spirit. It is repeated in Acts 2:17. I have heard churches with mighty moves of God say we are living in the last days, but the last days actually began 2,000 years ago when Jesus left so the Holy Spirit could come in the upper room! We are in the last days because 1,000 days on earth are like a single day in heaven, and a day in heaven is like a thousand on earth.[26] This fact should not be used as a fear tactic to urge people to get right with Jesus because He is coming tomorrow. No one knows the day or hour. We should always be ready and on guard. We could be living our last day here; life is but a vapor.

> And it shall come to pass afterward that I will pour out My Spirit on all flesh; your sons and your daughters shall prophesy, your old men shall dream dreams, your young men shall see visions. And also on My menservants and on My maidservants I will pour out My Spirit in those days. And I will show wonders in the heavens and in the earth: blood and fire and pillars of smoke. The sun shall be turned into darkness, and the moon into blood, before the coming of the great and awesome day of the Lord. And it shall come to pass that whoever calls on the name of the Lord shall be saved. For in Mount Zion and in Jerusalem there shall be deliverance,

26. See 2 Peter 3:8.

> as the Lord has said, among the remnant whom the Lord calls. (Joel 2:28-32)

> I will restore to you the years that the swarming locust has eaten, the crawling locust, the consuming locust, and the chewing locust, My great army which I sent among you. (Joel 2:25)

This is one of my favorite verses. It refers to the terrible army God sent in judgment against Israel, but it also speaks of God's restoration to His people. The next few verses though have a message that is for us as well:

> "Now, therefore," says the Lord, "turn to Me with all your heart, with fasting, with weeping, and with mourning." So rend your heart, and not your garments; return to the Lord your God, for He is gracious and merciful, slow to anger, and of great kindness; and He relents from doing harm. Who knows if He will turn and relent, and leave a blessing behind Him—a grain offering and a drink offering for the Lord your God? Blow the trumpet in Zion, consecrate a fast, call a sacred assembly; gather the people, sanctify the congregation, assemble the elders, gather the children and nursing babes; let the bridegroom go out from his chamber, and

> the bride from her dressing room. Let the priests, who minister to the Lord, weep between the porch and the altar; let them say, "Spare Your people, O Lord, and do not give Your heritage to reproach, that the nations should rule over them. Why should they say among the peoples, 'Where is their God?' " (Joel 2:12-17)

This is a new and different call to an army that is rising today. When I used to read this, I had focused so much on the restoration that I almost missed this army. Then the Spirit of the Lord impressed on me that it was time to assemble the army Joel mentioned above. Joel's army of warriors described above have sanctified themselves in intercession and repentance. Now is the time for them to rise up.

Everyone reading this has a warrior spirit inside. It has always been there. You need to wake it up; you have been quiet too long. Right now, wherever you are, let out a warrior cry!

Hallelujah!

Nice try, not even close. This is a warrior you are waking up. It has been dormant for years, so let out a *warrior* cry.

Hallelujah!

That was it.

You are a warrior. Never forget it. There is a fire before you and behind you blazing the way. You are called to be a trailblazer for the kingdom of God. We rend our hearts and not our garments. We walk humbly and listen to what the Lord would say to us. This is a description of the warrior army to which you belong. This multitude of warriors has never been seen before and never will be again. You are not alone. A throng of warriors is coming alongside you to destroy every stronghold that the Enemy has put on God's children. Strong are those who execute the Word of God. Now is the time to execute His Word. Now is the time for the rise of the warriors. We are to assemble and walk in the strength of the Lord.

> Let us hold fast the confession of our hope without wavering, for He who promised is faithful. And let us consider one another in order to stir up love and good works, not forsaking the assembling of ourselves together, as is the manner of some, but exhorting one another, and so much the more as you see the Day approaching. (Hebrews 10:23-25)

So now is the time. You sit in the valley of decision. Will you join up? Will you rise up in the warrior spirit that you are? You are not alone. God sees a warrior inside of you too. He placed it there. It is time that you see yourself like your Creator sees you.

God has spoken, "Rouse the warriors, prepare for holy war."

> Proclaim this among the nations: Prepare for holy war; rouse the warriors; let all the men of war advance and attack! (Joel 3:9 CSB)

Remember, there is no armor for your back. We are always advancing on the Enemy, never retreating. Advance and attack. Remember that the Enemy is terrified of the child of God who understands their identity in Christ. Even the weakest is stronger than the Enemy. When we are in Christ, let the weak say *I am strong.*

> Beat your plows into swords and your pruning knives into spears. Let even the weakling say, "I am a warrior." (Joel 3:10 CSB)

I am a warrior!

I'd like to end this chapter with a prophetic word I received just as this book was being edited. Here it is:

Prepare for War

The hour is here! Assemble My army. Rouse the Warriors. The fight against good and evil has been waged since the beginning of time. Demons have infiltrated behind our lines because My commanders have allowed it. Have I not already handed you the victory? Yet many still will not fight. My chosen ones will arise around the earth. The same ones whom some leaders have discounted. My chosen ones are those who have experienced unimaginable pain. This experience has birthed undeniable strength within them. My strength has been made perfect in their weakness. The anointing they carry will destroy and utterly obliterate the yoke. It is the same yoke with which many in the church have become comfortable and have refused to remove from My people. Too many have feared the Enemy more than Me. Many of those who lead are weak and show no courage, but My frontline warriors are beginning to emerge. Watch and see what I can do through them. They have looked up and have seen where their help comes from. I allowed all the evil of this time to be uncovered for this hour. My obedient servants who listen to My voice have the Holy Spirit to lead them. They have proven themselves worthy. They are tested by fire and purified like gold; My remnant is unstoppable. They do not retreat or break ranks. Their heart is after Mine. They have no agenda but the furthering of My kingdom. My glory shall manifest among them. My fire goes before them. The winds from the four corners of the earth blow forever in their favor. Joel's prophecy is being fulfilled at this very moment as these who walk in repentance and prayer first and foremost arise. Those who doubted My prophetic voice will to come to believe. Mighty signs and wonders are unveiling; My glorious deeds are being unleashed at this very moment. The midnight hour has come. I have heard My warriors' prayers and have come because of them. I will inhabit their praise and worship. Judah has come first! Now *fight!*

> Proclaim this among the nations: "Prepare for war! Wake up the mighty men, let all the men of war draw near, let them come up." (Joel 3:9)

About the Author

Sarah Davis is co-host of WOW Kingdom Conversations podcast and author of *Revelation Straight Out of Quarantine*. She is a single mother of two children and lives in Manassas, Virginia. Her vision is to see the Joshua generation take their full inheritance in the kingdom of God as sons and daughters.

Email: wowministers@yahoo.com

Instagram: wow__ministries

CPSIA information can be obtained
at www.ICGtesting.com
Printed in the USA
JSHW042147270222
23245JS00002B/9

9 780578 343631